To Be a Star

By Michele Spirn
Illustrated by Caroline Hu

Scott Foresman
is an imprint of

Glenview, Illinois • Boston, Massachusetts • Chandler, Arizona •
Upper Saddle River, New Jersey

Illustrations
Caroline Hu.

Photographs
Every effort has been made to secure permission and provide appropriate credit for photographic material. The publisher deeply regrets any omission and pledges to correct errors called to its attention in subsequent editions.

Unless otherwise acknowledged, all photographs are the property of Pearson Education, Inc.

20 Jose Hernandez/Corbis.

ISBN 13: 978-0-328-51952-1
ISBN 10: 0-328-51952-9

4 5 6 7 8 9 10 V0FL 15 14 13 12 11

Becky watched as Ms. Cohen looked over the class. She crossed her fingers and wished hard.

"Please, please pick me," she whispered to herself.

The teacher was choosing people to be in the class play. Ms. Cohen didn't really know the students in the class. She'd been asked to come in at the last minute to take over because Ms. Ryan was sick. Now she had to cast the play and put it on in just three weeks.

"Who thinks she can play Sara? There are a lot of lines to learn in a couple of weeks," the teacher said. "There's not much time, so we need someone with a great memory."

Becky's hand shot up first. Then she saw that Marta, her best friend, had raised her hand too.

"All right," said Ms. Cohen. "Because there are two of you, we'll have to draw lots for the part to be fair."

She wrote "Sara" on one scrap of paper, left the other piece of paper blank, and threw them both into a small bag. Marta picked out a scrap from the bag, and Becky drew the remaining paper after Marta. She opened her slip of paper. It said "Sara" in big letters.

"I got it!" Becky shouted.

"Do you think you can learn all the lines in time?" the teacher asked.

"No problem!" said Becky as she nodded her head.

Becky turned to Marta just as Marta put her head down. Becky realized that her friend had really wanted the part.

That afternoon the girls walked home from school together.

"I'm sorry you didn't get the part," Becky said. "I know that you're a really good actress."

"That's okay," said Marta. "I'm going to like playing the part of Mary. It'll be fun acting with you. Sara and Mary have a lot of scenes together."

"I'm so excited," Becky said. "My parents are going to be in shock that I'm in a play. I've always told them that I never wanted to act."

"How come?" asked Marta.

"Acting always looked so hard. I've never been sure I would be good at it," Becky said.

"I thought acting talent ran in your family," Marta said. "Your grandfather was a famous actor, right?"

Becky sighed. "That's the problem. Everyone thinks if my grandfather can act, I must be able to act too. That's why I've stayed away from it. Now, I think I am finally brave enough to try acting. I'll work hard and practice a lot, but we'll see how I do."

"I'm sure you'll be great," Marta said. "I'll help you."

That night Becky started studying her lines. She was busy trying to memorize them when her mother knocked on her bedroom door.

"How's it going?" her mother asked.

Becky groaned. "It's going so slowly. This is a hard play."

"What's it about?" her mother asked.

"It's about what the settlers went through when they came to America. Life was really difficult. There was a drought so there wasn't enough water for plants to grow. All the grass dried up, and the sheep had nothing to graze on."

"It sounds interesting," her mother said. "What's making the play so hard for you?"

"Well, I play Sara, one of the first settlers. It's so sad because her parents died on the ship, and she came to a new land all alone. I have to act with a lot of emotion and feeling, and on top of that, she has so many lines!"

"Do you want me to practice with you, honey?" her mother asked.

"Yeah, Mom, that would be great. Thanks!" Becky pointed to her script as she continued. "This is the part where the Native Americans welcome us to a ceremonial feast. This is the first time we have seen so much food since we left the old country.

"I say, 'Thank you for welcoming us with such abundance. We are very grateful for your generosity.'"

"It sounds like you know your lines," said her mother. "But maybe you could seem a little more excited to see so much food. After all, Sara and the others must have been very hungry."

Becky tried her lines again. When she looked up her mother was making a funny face.

"Hmm. That doesn't seem quite right either. Maybe your father can help," she said as she called his name.

Becky's dad walked up the stairs.

"What's going on?" he asked.

"Becky needs some help with her lines," replied her mother.

"Oh, so you need some help memorizing them?" Becky's dad asked.

"No, that's not it," Becky said. "I know my lines just fine, but I don't know *how* to say them.

"When I say the lines, it sounds like I'm just reading words from a book. It doesn't sound like it's what I really feel," Becky explained.

Becky's dad thought for a minute.

Then he said, "Show me your lines, Becky. I've got an idea."

Becky's father skimmed the script, and then he handed it back to Becky as he looked around her room.

"First, it helps to be in costume," he said.

He found an old scarf and wound it around his head. He threw one of Becky's sweaters over his shoulders.

"Now I feel like Mary," he said.

"You look so silly!" Becky laughed as she and her mother fell into a fit of giggles.

"Excuse me, I'm acting," said her father, pretending to be offended. Then he said Mary's lines in a high, squeaky voice and gestured wildly, exaggerating all of his movements. At the same time, he threw his hands up and stepped back with a pleased look on his face.

"Look how pleased I am to see the food," he said. "Now you try it."

Becky tried it again.

Almost immediately she started to get frustrated.

"I can't do it as well as you can," she said. "It's too hard. I feel silly acting as if I'm happy to see all that food. It's not even real food!"

"You have to pretend," her father said. "That's what all actors do. It's sort of like when you and your friends play pretend games. Forget that you're Becky. Try pretending that you're Sara. I know you can do it. I'm sure the teacher wouldn't have given you the part if she didn't think you could do it."

"She just picked me because we drew lots for the part. Marta is a much better actress. She should have gotten the part," said Becky.

"You have the part now, so you should practice it," her father said.

Becky tried again. She threw down the script. "This just isn't working!" she cried.

Her father patted her on the shoulder.

"It's hard, but you'll get it," he said. "Acting takes a lot of work and practice. Look at Grandpa! He acted for years before people started paying him to do it."

Becky listened to her father and nodded. Unfortunately, she didn't have years. Her play was in just a few weeks!

"Don't forget, we're going to Grandpa's house tonight," her father reminded her. "Maybe he can help you. He certainly knows a lot about acting."

After dinner with her grandfather, Becky looked at all the pictures in his scrapbook. They were many pictures of her grandfather acting in different roles. Becky asked him how he came to be such a good actor.

"I practiced, but I didn't start out with big parts. I took little parts and practiced until I got good enough to get the big ones," he said.

"Did you ever think you might not be good?" Becky asked.

"Many times, but I really wanted to act, so I stuck with it," he said.

"What if you thought someone else might be better at the part?" Becky asked.

"That's a tough one," her grandfather said. "Sometimes to be a star you have to think of the good of the play. Maybe the play would be better off with someone else playing your part. I did that once. I switched parts with someone, and the play was a big success."

"Were people disappointed that you weren't the star?" Becky asked.

"Not really," her grandfather said. "Remember, it's more important to feel good about what you do than care about what others think of you."

That night, before Becky went to sleep, she read her part again. She kept thinking about what her grandfather had said.

To be a star you have to think of the good of the play, he had told her. *It's more important to feel good about what you do than care about what others think of you....*

She fell asleep dreaming about the play. Becky dreamed that she had forgotten her lines. She was alone on stage, and no one could help her. She tried to open her mouth, but no words came out. Finally, she ran off the stage, and the dream ended.

She woke up even more nervous than before! She didn't want to mess up in front of everyone!

The next day was the last one before the play.
Becky stood against the painted backdrop of the
feast and said her lines.

"Can you say your lines with a little more
emotion, Becky?" Ms. Cohen asked.

Becky felt herself getting frustrated again. She
was trying as hard as she could. She really didn't
know what else to do. "Maybe Marta could help
you," Ms. Cohen suggested.

Marta practiced the lines with Becky. Becky
could see just how good of an actress Marta was.
Now Becky was sure that Marta would be better
than she was as the star of the play.

That afternoon, Becky talked to Marta. Then both of them went to see Ms. Cohen. Their teacher listened to both girls talk. She thought for a minute.

"I am surprised," she said. "It's a bit close to the show to be doing something like this, but if both of you girls think it will work, I'll go along with it. I will trust you."

Then Becky went to Marta's house, and they both practiced their lines.

"Much better," said Becky. "You sound good."

"So do you," said Marta. "Thanks for everything, Becky."

The next day was the day of the play. Becky and Marta got ready. They waited on the stage. Becky peeked out of the curtains and saw her parents walk into the auditorium. Then she got a surprise. Her grandfather was standing right next to them.

"I want to see my granddaughter, the star," she could hear him saying to everyone.

Becky's heart beat fast. Could she go through with what she had planned? Would her parents still be proud of her? What would her grandfather think? Then she remembered what her grandfather had said: *It's more important that you feel good about what you do than what others think of you.*

Becky smiled. Her parents and her grandfather were in for a surprise.

Just then, the lights in the auditorium dimmed, and everyone in the audience got very quiet.

"Ooh, quiet! I think it's starting," said Becky's mom. "I think Becky's in the first scene!"

Ms. Cohen came on stage first.

"I am proud to present our play, "A Year in America." All of the students have worked hard to make this play a success. You can see their names in the program. We have one change to tell you about. The part of Sara will be played by Marta Andres, and the part of Mary will be played by Becky Samuels."

Becky's parents looked at each other confused.

"Did you know about this?" her father asked. Becky's mother shook her head. She was as confused as everyone else. Her grandfather just smiled to himself quietly.

When Becky came out on stage, she said her lines and then looked for her grandfather. What would he think? Had she done the right thing by changing roles with Marta?

At the end of the play, she bowed with the rest of the students. Then she saw her grandfather standing up to clap.

Afterwards, her parents came up to Becky.

"That was a surprise! Why did you change parts with Marta?" her father asked.

"That's because Becky knows what it is to be a real star," her grandfather said. Then he winked at Becky, and she winked back.

Women and Acting

People have been acting in plays for thousands of years. The first actors were in Greece around 2,500 years ago. These actors were men. Women were not allowed to act on stage in ancient Greece.

This was also true in other places in the world. In England, men had to act the women's parts until the 1600s. At that time, people thought that actors were not trustworthy. They didn't want women to be around people like that.

Now, of course, both men and women are actors. Acting in plays, movies, and television is something that many people want to do.